CHAKRAS for STARTERS

❖

Unlock the Hidden Doors to Peace and Well-Being

Savitri Simpson

BASED ON THE TEACHINGS OF

J. DONALD WALTERS

Crystal Clarity Publishers
Nevada City, CA

ISBN: 1-56589-156-2

Cover photo by J. Donald Walters
Cover design by C. A. Starner Schuppe

Printed in Canada

CRYSTAL

CLARITY

Crystal Clarity Publishers
14618 Tyler-Foote Road
Nevada City, CA 95959

Phone: 800-424-1055
Website: www.crystalclarity.com
E-mail: clarity@crystalclarity.com

Library of Congress Cataloging-in-Publication Data

Simpson, Savitri, 1950-
   Chakras for starters : unlock the hidden door to peace and well-being
/ Savitri Simpson ; based on the teachings of J. Donald Walters.
      p. cm.
   ISBN 1-56589-156-2
   1. Chakra (Hinduism) 2. Meditation--Hinduism. 3. Yoga. I. Walters,
J. Donald. II. Title.
   BL1215.C45 S55 2002
   131--dc21

                                                              2002010815

More praise for *Chakras for Starters*:

Chakras for Starters is a succinct but power-packed presentation. Simpson restores the essential spiritual understanding of each of the chakras; this book is a valuable tool for seekers on the path. The meditations and exercises she presents for each chakra brings the material out of the conceptual and into practice.

—David Pond, author of *Chakras for Beginners* and
Astrology and Relationships

Chakras for Starters is not only rich in information about the chakras, it offers techniques that can help you learn how to tap into these energetic bridges that connect the physical with the spiritual…bridges that will change the way you see yourself and others forever.

—Carol Ritberger Ph.D. author of *Your Personality, Your Health*

Chakras for Starters is the one truly essential book on the chakras that I have read. In this clear, easy-to-understand presentation, Savitri Simpson tells you exactly what you need to know about the chakras and how to work with them for your own upliftment and spiritual growth. I highly recommend it.

—Jyotish Novak, author of *How to Meditate*

Contents

❖

Contents

Contents

Acknowledgments

❖

Much of the material in *Chakras for Starters* is based on the books, lessons, and audio tapes of J. Donald Walters. For over fifty years, Mr. Walters (for myself and many others he is known as Swami Kriyananda) has been lecturing and writing on yoga, meditation, and other related spiritual topics. He is a direct disciple of the great yogi master, Paramhansa Yogananda, upon whose teaching this book and all of his works are based. The subject of the chakras and how they work appears in many of his lectures and books; but until now, they have never been brought together in one place.

For the past 26 years I have had the great privilege of being Donald Walters' student, striving to absorb his teaching and through him the teachings of his (and my) guru, Paramhansa Yogananda, reading all his books, studying his lessons, and listening to every tape I could "un-earth" from the massive Ananda archives. Swami Kriyananda's teachings on the chakras are truly remarkable in their clarity, humor, and practicality; in these teachings he has been able to present some of the deeper

9

and more esoteric teachings of yoga in a way which is simple and easily applicable to one's daily life. It has been my great honor and joy to help bring *Chakras for Starters* into existence.

I would like to thank the following people for their help in this project: Jyotish and Devi Novak, Julie Morgan, Sean Meshorer, Cathy Parojinog, Roy Gugliotta, Alan Heubert, Peter and Nirmala Schuppe, Sarah Brink, and my husband, Sudarshan Simpson, along with all my fellow gurubais, friends, and students on the path of Self-realization.

I offer this book with love and humility at the feet of the Omnipresent Spirit, which is within us all.

Savitri Simpson
Ananda Village
Nevada City, California

Introduction

❖

"Seek ye first the kingdom of God, and his righteousness; and all these things shall be added unto you." (Matthew 6:37) These oft-quoted words of Jesus are central to his message to his disciples and to the whole world. When questioned by the Pharisees as to where this kingdom might be found or when it would manifest on earth, Jesus replies: "Behold, the kingdom of God is within you." (Luke 17:21)

We may be as confused right now as Jesus' listeners were so long ago. How do you "seek within" and where exactly is this "inner kingdom"? A look inside our physical bodies would not show us anything that might be called the "kingdom of God," even though our human bodies are magnificently created and worthy of awe. Yet we all sense that there is something else going on within ourselves—something beyond flesh and blood, corpuscles and teardrops.

Once, while the great yoga master Paramhansa Yogananda was speaking to his students he paused to say: "O, if only you could see yourself as I see you. I can see beyond the flesh and entrails, when the light comes. It is so beautiful!" This "light body" of which Yogananda speaks is also called the astral body, of which the chakras are key components.

In addition to offering information about the chakras, this book includes guided meditations and experiential exercises for each chakra, for it is important for the chakras to be experienced internally as well as being understood intellectually.

May God's light and blessings fill you completely and bless your inner journey toward final freedom and oneness with all that is.

CHAKRAS
for STARTERS

The Seven Chakras

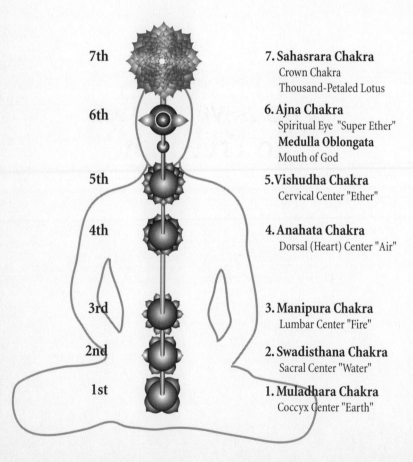

7th

7. Sahasrara Chakra
Crown Chakra
Thousand-Petaled Lotus

6th

6. Ajna Chakra
Spiritual Eye "Super Ether"
Medulla Oblongata
Mouth of God

5th

5. Vishudha Chakra
Cervical Center "Ether"

4th

4. Anahata Chakra
Dorsal (Heart) Center "Air"

3rd

3. Manipura Chakra
Lumbar Center "Fire"

2nd

2. Swadisthana Chakra
Sacral Center "Water"

1st

1. Muladhara Chakra
Coccyx Center "Earth"

CHAPTER ONE

❖

The Seven Gates to Freedom

"Who is in my temple?
All the doors do open themselves,
All the lights do light themselves,
Darkness like a dark bird,
Flies away, O flies away."

—From a poem by Rabindranath Tagore, set to
music by Paramhansa Yogananda in *Cosmic
Chants,* 1938

What Is a Chakra?

Chakra is a Sanskrit word literally meaning wheel or circle. In a deeper sense the word describes the whirlpools or vortices of energy located along the central axis of our bodies, in the "deep" or astral spine. The chakras are a part of what might be called our spiritual anatomy. Just as there is an anatomy to the physical body and maps to the physical world, so also there is a definite anatomy of our spiritual beings, as well as maps and guideposts to follow along the path of inner awakening. If we understand this spiritual anatomy, then we will find it much easier to advance in our search for God.

For example, the point between the eyebrows (the sixth chakra) is that part of the body where the mind becomes focused automatically in ecstasy or just in concentration. Perhaps you've noticed the unconscious tendency people have to knit their brows, or frown, when engrossed in a project or making an important point in conversation. Understanding this truth, and consciously putting our attention at that point, we discover that the mind actually does become focused there. This is one of the central teachings of yoga.

Yoga is a continuous tradition of teachings and techniques

that help the ascending soul to understand that there are higher levels of consciousness that transcend lower levels of awareness. Generally speaking, information about the chakras comes from India and from the ancient science of yoga. Yoga is a true and universal teaching, yet yoga does not have a corner on truth. Anyone who finds spiritual freedom or oneness with God, no matter whether they are from an Eastern or Western background, discovers the same truths. Yoga's unique value lies in its scientific approach to finding God, based on an ancient tradition of experimentation. It offers nonsectarian guidance and wisdom for those seeking higher awareness, based on centuries of experience.

Spiritual awakening is not a vague, mystical experience. All true teachings, although some less specifically than yoga, point to very particular realities. As an example of this, we find statements in every scripture that say that heaven is "above" and hell is "below." But no telescope has ever shown us angels flying around in outer space. Nor has any deep well-drilling equipment brought up screaming and protesting demons. Heaven and hell are not "up" and "down" objectively speaking—what is up for us is down for people in Australia. This concept has no cosmic relevance, but it does have infinite relevance for the individual.

We can easily see this relevance in our instinctive responses to life. When we feel uplifted or high, or downcast or low, we use expressions which reflect these feelings. Spiritual awakening implies raising of energy and consciousness in the body. And hellish consciousness, materialistic consciousness—that which takes us away from joy and down into suffering and pain—is always a descent. Isn't it true that every time we feel wonderful, we experience a rising energy inside ourselves, and we look up?

You never see people smiling and looking upward, saying, "I feel so depressed." Likewise, you don't see people slumping, looking down and droopy, saying "I feel so happy." Quite the contrary, for these physical reactions are manifestations of universal truths, based on the way we are made. What yoga does is particularize these truths by showing that outer experiences of joy or sadness are caused by energy moving in the deep spine. But yoga doesn't teach this concept as a dogma. It says: "Try it! Experience it!" For everyone who has tried it, has experienced it.

When our energy is uplifted in the spine we begin to approach divine consciousness. But in the beginning of our spiritual quest, we encounter what might be called "gates" or "doors" (words often used to describe the seven chakras) that need to be unlocked.

Locating the Chakras

The spinal centers, or chakras, are found at the points where tributary streams of energy (*prana* or life force) from the body join the upward flow of energy in the deep or astral spine. The astral, or energy, spine is not the backbone (those knobs that can be felt along the back), but runs more or less through the center of the body. Energy flows through the central nervous system and through the astral spine. In our un-awakened state, the main energy-flow is downward, away from the brain, and outward to the organs and limbs.

The chakras correspond to the spinal plexuses in the physical body, from which nerves branch out to provide energy to the different body parts. As we go deeper in meditation and prayer, uplifting our consciousness, the energy begins to flow upward in the spine. Try to feel this internal "river of life" at your center as the location of the chakras.

First Chakra: The first chakra is located at the base of the spine. It is also called the *muladhara,* or coccyx center. From this center radiate the nerves that go to the lower parts of the body: the anus, and the legs.

Second Chakra: An inch and a half above the first chakra is the *swadisthana,* or sacral center. The nerves from this center operate the reproductive system.

Third Chakra: Opposite the navel in the astral spine is the *manipura,* or lumbar center, the nerves from which operate the digestive system and all the internal organs and glands in the abdominal cavity (spleen, liver, kidneys, adrenals, etc.).

Fourth Chakra: At the region of the heart in the spine is the *anahata,* or dorsal center, from which nerves radiate out to the heart, lungs, and chest, and into the arms and hands.

Fifth Chakra: The *vishudha,* or cervical center, from which nerves radiate to the throat, neck, and vocal chords, is opposite the throat in the spine.

Sixth Chakra: The highest spinal center is located in the medulla oblongata, at the base of the brain just above the place where the skull connects with the neck. Its positive pole is the *ajna* chakra, at the point between the eyebrows. The medulla oblongata is the center through which cosmic energy feeds the entire body with *prana* (life force or conscious cosmic energy).

Seventh Chakra: The *sahasrara* chakra, is located in the cranium, at the top of the head. This center is traditionally known as the thousand-petaled lotus, or crown chakra.

Functions of the Chakras

In addition to their physical functions, the chakras store and distribute energy and information. They also serve as the location of our psychological or mental tendencies, habits, and desires. In fact, the astral spine is a long, downward extension of the subconscious mind. Our inner struggle to grow and change spiritually takes place between the pull of the soul from above and the pull of matter and material involvement from below.

Every unfulfilled desire, every wave of like or dislike, every karmic action, creates a subtle vortex of energy. These energy vortices are held together by centripetal thoughts, such as: "I want this; I reject that; I like this; I don't like that; this is what I have done; that is what I failed to accomplish." The ego hugs these thoughts and impulses to itself until they gain release outwardly in action, or inwardly in self-realization. To work out all desires or karma in the outer world is, ultimately, not feasible, for out of every fulfilled desire there arise two, or twenty, or a hundred other new desires.

These vortices of desire, also called *vrittis,* enter the sub-conscious and sink to their respective levels in the spine in the area of a specific chakra, according to the relative grossness or refinement of the energy they express. Their location in the spine depends on the chakra with which their vibrations are in harmony ("like attracts like"). The more spiritual a vortex, the higher the center around which it settles; the more materialis-tic a vortex, the lower the center. Very old vortices, as yet unre-solved, are submerged, so to speak, by more recently created vortices, and have little or no effect on the waking conscious-ness. They continue, however, like little ripples on the surface of larger waves, to obscure the clear reflection of the Eternal Spirit, long after the larger waves of the initial desire or feeling have subsided.

The energy of these vortices, when released to flow up-ward, combines to produce a mighty river of energy before which no obstacle can stand. A strong upward flow of energy in the spine dissolves those vortices automatically, just as a strong flow of water in a river dissolves the little eddies along its banks. Thus an increase of the flow of energy inward and upward through the astral spine is a major tool for awakening and unlocking the chakra "gates."

The Chakras and the Elements

One helpful system for understanding the chakras is through the "elements." In the yogic teachings there are five primary elements: earth, water, fire, air, and ether (always given in that relative sequence). These are not elements in the sense that a chemist would use the term, but in a more spiritual sense. They represent stages of manifestation outward from Spirit to matter.

If we think of ether as representing the primordial energy out of which the first atoms were born, of air as representing the nebulous gases, fire the stars, water the molten state of matter as it cools still further, and earth as matter that has cooled sufficiently to become solid, we find that those particular "elements" very clearly epitomize the elemental stages of creation.

These elements also describe the stages of the soul's descent into matter, and, when reversed, the progressive stages of its liberation. In the process of entering the physical body, the consciousness hypnotizes itself into thinking that it has become a body made of solid matter. To break this hypnosis, one must identify with the inner soul. We will find it easier to retrace our steps God-ward if, instead of denying Divine Spirit in the lower elemental manifestations, we draw what divine understanding we can from *every* manifestation. For God truly has become everything. It is our perception that must be purified to behold the Divine Spirit everywhere.

As we retrace our consciousness from matter to Spirit, we reverse the route by which we first came into physical form. We follow definite stages of awakening in our awareness of who and what we really are. Thus, the "story" of our evolution—and in truth the story of the manifestation of all creation in its various stages, from Spirit to matter—is indelibly imprinted in our astral anatomy, waiting for us to discover its presence within and then follow that divine pathway back from matter to pure consciousness. The elements of earth, water, fire, air, and ether, (also super-ether, a state beyond even space itself), represent an orderly progression of steps on the path which we must all inevitably follow—a path to oneness and final freedom in God.

In the following chapters, the helpful symbols of the elements are used to clarify the nature and essence of each individual chakra.

CHAPTER TWO

❖

The Earth Element (First Chakra)

"Some men lack the daring,
Ever to be free,
They shun the heights, and cloud the depths,
And court security.

Come, you're a man, no passive stone!
Stand up, and call your soul your own!
Banish weakness: Go on alone!
Don't look back: Just go on alone!"

—"Truth Can Never Die!"
    from *Songs of Divine Joy*, by Swami Kriyananda

Steadfastness, Endurance, and Faith

The first chakra in its positive aspects helps us to learn to concentrate, to persevere, and to cling to truth. Only then may we offer these qualities inward and upward into a flowing vision, which makes it possible to adapt to change at a moment's notice. If the energy is misdirected in this chakra, then we are too stubborn, too hard, or inflexible. Thus, the same quality, which in a positive context is very helpful to our spiritual growth, becomes a detriment if it's directed downward or outward toward the world. People who are too hardheaded, too bigoted, too harsh, or too firm with others, are affirming the delusion of separateness from God, from life, and from other people. In short, they're affirming their egos. Everything that is inimical to spiritual growth is being emphasized in their minds when they think that way.

Attachment to things, to people, to getting our way, is another negative aspect of this chakra—even attachment to goodness and beauty. We are attached to beautiful things partly because they are solid as well as beautiful—we can touch them and feel them. The love of beauty is a spiritual quality, but it can take us into delusion if we add to it the wish to own it, touch it, and feel it—in other words, if we add to it the earth element of solidity.

Notice how, the greater a person's attachment to "solid realities," the more set his own outlook becomes on life; and how, conversely, the more stolidly materialistic a person, the more his tastes incline to solid, heavy objects: big cars, solid walls in his home, thick, plush furnishings, heavy foods. Mentally, too, he is inclined to have a "heavy" outlook on life—to be dogmatic, set in his ways, and rather dull. He is worldly not only because of his attachment to the things of this world, but even more because of a certain heavy earthiness in his own consciousness.

Our earthiness must be dealt with at its elemental source. If we can overcome all inflexibility and mental "heaviness" in ourselves, the solid properties of objective matter will cease to attract us. For us to rise above these qualities, however, before we have learned their positive lessons, may be as premature as putting a child behind the wheel of a car before he has learned how to use the brake.

Remember that the first chakra's earth "element" has important spiritual teachings to impart to us. The tendency to remain set in our ways can be developed into steadfastness in our search for truth. Stolidity can become even-minded endurance in the face of life's dualities such as heat and cold, pleasure and pain, joy and sorrow. Dogmatism can become true faith, born of a desire to experience truth directly and thereby truly to know. Even heaviness of mind has its divine aspect, for it can be purified into stability, or a consciousness of being always firmly centered in the Higher Self.

Loyalty: The First Law of God

Paramhansa Yogananda often said, "Loyalty is the first law of God." We can understand an expression like "the first law of God" in two ways: we can take it as the highest law, or we can take it as the first law. In the present context it would be wise to understand it in the second way, for loyalty is an essential quality for spiritual growth. Loyalty is a positive aspect of this first chakra.

On the other side of the coin (and there is always another side!), in India they say: "It is no doubt a blessing to be born into a religion, but it is a misfortune to die in one." This means that firmness of purpose should be offered up into a breadth of mind, an expansive vision.

In organizations or religions we hear a lot about the importance of loyalty. But it is usually stated in such a way that the member has to be loyal to the organization. The way

Paramhansa Yogananda put it was the other way around. First and foremost he was loyal to his disciples, and it was because of *his* loyalty to them that they were loyal to him. This kind of commitment is absolutely necessary: to be loyal to your friends so that no matter what they do, you will always love and help them.

Swami Kriyananda tells of a person who once tried diligently to convert him to another path. "I finally said to this man, 'Listen, I'm not going to argue the relative merits of our two paths, because I don't want to argue against your faith. I don't want to undermine your faith, and I certainly don't want to surrender my faith. So let's put it this way: Maybe your path is better than mine, since that's what you want to say; but I wouldn't be comfortable in your path. I'm comfortable with mine. If it's a second best path, it's still *my* path.' He couldn't say anything after that."

Swami Kriyananda continued: "I'm loyal to my mother. She's a wonderful woman. I haven't any doubt that there are plenty of women in the world who are more wonderful. But I'm not running around looking for better mothers. I'm perfectly satisfied with my own."

We have to have that kind of commitment to our own family and friends, our spiritual teacher, our spiritual path, and our purpose in life. Then we are aligning ourselves with the first chakra's positive quality of loyalty to truth, which is the basis upon which all other spiritual qualities begin to grow.

Although our goal is to lift our energy up through the astral spine and the chakras to the spiritual eye, it is not wrong to meditate and feel yourself centered in each of the lower chakras first. Indeed, it is very helpful, as long as you are doing so in order first to be aware of them and then to stimulate their flow inward and upward.

Meditation for the First Chakra

Try meditating on the earth element. Sit upright and close your eyes. Hold your body very still. Feel that you are a rock—absolutely immovable, stable, and firm.

It may even help you to have a rock or a crystal that appeals to you in its shape, its size and its color—something that you can touch and look at as you practice this meditation. Hold it, feel its firmness, and take that sense of communion with whatever you like about it into yourself. Or, if you are able to, go somewhere in nature and sit on a large boulder or rock outcropping, perhaps beside or in a river. Sit still and feel the strength of the boulder beneath you, unshakable, though the rivers of change swirl all around you. Even if you can't physically be in a place like this, go there in your imagination. Consciously draw these feelings and attitudes into yourself.

Repeat mentally several times: "I am steadfast, determined, unshakably loyal to truth. I endure all things with calm faith in God."

As you continue to meditate, don't allow a single muscle to move. Feel the weight of your body pressing down into the chair, the floor, the earth, boulder, or whatever you're sitting on. The weight of gravity pulls you so firmly to the earth that you couldn't move if you tried. Now turn that consciousness of firmness, of physical solidity, into determination and fixity of purpose (this is an excellent attitude to adopt at the beginning of every meditation). Concentrate in the coccyx center as you look upward toward the point between the eyebrows. Mentally chant AUM (pronounced "Om") at that chakra and direct its energy upward to the spiritual eye. Inhale and lift your consciousness and focus it at the point between the eyebrows.

Now close your meditation by mentally affirming: "I am firm in my purpose. I want only Thee. I want only Thee."

CHAPTER THREE

❖

The Water Element (Second Chakra)

"Leave home in the sunshine,
And dance through a meadow,
Or sit by a stream and just be;
The lilt of the water,
Will gather your worries,
And carry them down to the sea."

—"There's Joy in the Heavens,"
  from *Songs of Divine Joy*, by Swami Kriyananda

Flowing with Life's Changes

If we are to develop the positive aspect of each chakra, we need always to take their energy inward and then offer it upward. For example, the qualities of steadfast loyalty and firmness of purpose of the first chakra are only perfected when they are offered into the second chakra, the fluid or water element. Inner stability, though a good quality in itself, will lead to mental ossification if it is not allied to a more fluid consciousness, symbolized by water.

The second chakra is located about an inch and a half above the first chakra, which is at the base of the spine. This is the chakra controlling sexual energy, procreation and expansion of the species. This same expansiveness turned inward leads to creativity in all forms, open-mindedness, and the ability to be receptive to new ideas and divine inspirations.

The water element exemplifies a flowing kind of consciousness that is attached to nothing. A river, for example, isn't bound by any place; it just keeps on moving toward the sea. This positive or beneficial aspect of the second chakra gives us the ability to flow naturally though life. Without an ability to move with the currents of grace, spiritual growth would be difficult. Yet this more flowing awareness, when it is directed outwardly toward mere things, constitutes the second elemental cause of our attachment to this world. For it is not only the solidity or "touch-ability" of material objects, but also, more subtly, their infinite variety that keeps us bound to them. If we can overcome the desire for change for its own sake—if, in other words, we can accept change when it comes, yet even in the midst of it remain even-minded—our sense of inner freedom from attachments will increase immeasurably.

The flowing freedom of a person in whom the earth and water elements have been brought into ideal harmony is like that of a skillful surfboarder. He can calmly ride the crest of every wave of change and direct himself wherever he wants to go, instead of being tossed and buffeted about, and perhaps ultimately broken, when conditions on which he has depended crash around him.

Life disappoints us in myriad ways and takes many things away from us. A negative attitude may come from seeing that life is not always going to give us what we want. Thus many people become bitter and disillusioned. But, in fact, a very wholesome and important step on the path to spiritual maturity is to learn how to relate to these realities. Death, bereavement, betrayal, people leaving us, failure—all of these losses have for their ultimate purpose our understanding that true reality is something greater. That is, we should not seek reality in form, but in the Infinite.

A monk Swami Kriyananda knew many years ago exemplifies this concept of learning to flow with life's challenges. In India the old tradition was that Hindu monks would travel about without money or possessions. Wherever they went villagers took care of them, giving them food and perhaps some shelter, which was all they wanted. The villagers felt it was a blessing to have these wandering *sadhus* passing through, sharing a little bit of their experience, inspiration, and wisdom.

Then, when modern times came, there was some crossover and confusion between the two eras. Monks began to take trains more frequently. For a while it was understood and accepted that, because of the old tradition, they would travel for free. However, sometimes a railroad company would decide not to honor this tradition.

One day this monk was traveling by train, but he had paid for his ticket. As he was walking confidently through the gate towards the waiting train, the ticket collector, assuming he was one of those freeloading monks, grabbed him roughly, to keep him from boarding.

Imagine how you might react to such an unjust physical

assault! Probably very few of us would have reacted the way this monk did, which was to simply relax and accept what was happening. He was so free in his consciousness that, from one second to the next, he was able to adapt to a new reality, and the shape of that reality didn't matter to him at all.

The water element in our consciousness—the ability to flow with life's constant changes—will help us find that kind of inner freedom.

"Wishy-washy-ness"

If, however, we develop in ourselves the more "watery" qualities of human nature—an easy-going, accommodative attitude—before acquiring the solid virtues of the earth element, then we may become wishy-washy, irresolute, or helplessly indecisive. To be dogmatic is, in itself, a human failing, but it is not good on the other hand to be so open-minded that one's brains fall out!

A negative side of the water element stage is this "wishy-washy" attitude. We see this quality in people who can't make up their minds about anything, who never really settle down. They take up a job and, before they can get anywhere with it, they decide to change it. Or they encounter some little obstacle in their path, and they decide this means that God doesn't want them to go in the direction they had chosen.

Swami Kriyananda once knew two women who exhibited this trait. They felt that everything that happened to them had to be a sign of God telling them what to do. For example, they would be all set to go out shopping, when of them would trip over the edge of a carpet while walking down the stairs. They would take this as a sign that they weren't supposed to go out, so they would stay home that day.

A tendency to be swayed by other people's opinions or desires is another aspect of this too-adaptive tendency. There are a lot of people on the spiritual path who suddenly wake up to the fact—and it is a fact—that being a devotee puts one in the minority. They realize that, as Krishna says in the Bhagavad Gita, "Only one out of a thousand seeks God." Becoming aware of this, they might think: "Well, gosh, I'm really out of it! Here I am foolishly chanting God's name, when everybody else out there is hustling for a dollar. What's wrong with me?"

Or perhaps they've been sneered at by relatives, who accuse them of impracticality and wasting their lives. There are many such devotees who then decide to go the way of the world and get this starry-eyed idea that they're going to become rich, or famous, or they're going to settle down in suburbia with a re-spectable home and job. But in doing so they leave their resolve to grow spiritually. When you look in their eyes a year or so later, they look dead and uninterested in life.

Thus we find that people who let themselves be swept along in the negative aspect of this watery element are seldom able to stand firm to their own principles. They are not able to be strong in their ideals, in their opinions, or in their directions. Their lack of steadfastness becomes a habitual way of thinking, and it is a great flaw.

True Discrimination

Another aspect of the water element urges us to learn true discrimination or discernment. Discrimination, really, should be applied primarily to yourself. It is important to be able to determine right from wrong in order to see how we hurt ourselves, and how others might be harming themselves. The value of recognizing negative behavior in others lies in absorbing knowledge for ourselves—seeing that adopting that behavior would be self-destructive. We don't want to judge anybody—there's a big difference between true discrimination and being judgmental. The best response to the negative acts of others is compassion for them.

When you hurt somebody else, you really hurt yourself much more. When you are truly able to give love to another person—even when they're wrong, even when they abuse you or others, even when they're unkind—you will find even more reason to love them, not less.

It is essential to develop that positive, loving attitude, because everything is at stake where our well being is concerned. When we have negative attitudes, we feel down and depressed about everything. It isn't that we're unhappy about anything specific, we're just down—period. And when we feel right about things, we're up—period.

So we need to develop every excuse and every reason we can think of to try to see goodness—in everything and everyone—but not out of blind ignorance or lack of discrimination. When we see a wrong in this world, we should try to right it, if it's within our power to do so. But at the same time we should do it in a positive way, not in a destructive or angry way.

Swami Kriyananda tells of how utterly respectful Yogananda was toward everyone. "It was so beautiful to see the respect that he gave utter fools, because he saw that God was playing a role there. That didn't mean he couldn't have a good laugh. Sure, he could laugh at the folly of this world. He often said, 'Divine Mother has a good sense of humor about what goes on in this world. She laughs about it, too.'"

Don't think God doesn't have a sense of humor. It doesn't show much discrimination not to be able to laugh at things. But it is important to laugh *with* people instead of *at* them. We need to be able to see things as they are, and ourselves as we are. But even while recognizing the imperfections and problems of this world, we can still see that God is in everything.

Paramhansa Yogananda once heard a group of people talking about the foibles of various others. His humorous comment was: "Well, why be astonished? After all, this whole world is just God's zoo." What a lovely comedy God has created here!

"And yet," Kriyananda says, "I never saw anyone more cheerful and positive about people than he was. You might remember the story I told in my autobiography, *The Path,* about a man who was performing a one-man dance recital. He was playing the part of a dying deer and also the part of the hunter. Master and I were laughing till the tears were streaming down our cheeks. We were both trying to laugh silently, but at one point I let out a louder laugh than I should have, and Master said quietly (choked with laughter himself) 'Don't, no-o-o . . . .'

"Later after the show ended, the man came to talk to Master. He was outraged at his mistreatment, because a sympathetic (to the audience) stagehand lowered the curtain before he'd finished his endless victory dance. Master had just finished laughing his heart out over this man's absurd performance, but now Yogananda saw he was really hurt and indignant.

"Master said gently and sympathetically: 'That's all right. I understand.' And he did, too. He understood all aspects of the matter. He wasn't being insincere, he was this man's friend! He wasn't laughing at the man. He was laughing at what the man did, and certainly not to his face."

We don't want to hate the sinner, no matter how much we dislike the sin. There should always be that differentiation between the soul that is perfect, and the stupid things the soul can get into when it thinks it's imperfect. We must strive for the ability to be real and see things as they are, but still not judge.

Yogananda didn't dislike that man because he seemed foolish. He loved him. He loved everyone! But he could laugh and sympathize about the same episode and still be absolutely sincere. So we all should be.

See everything in the light of God, but recognize that God,

too, is having fun. It's fine to recognize the absurdities of life—this attitude will give you a certain perspective that will be very beneficial. But always try to see the goodness in people and in life. Always try to see the struggling soul learning through its mistakes.

Intuition and Inner Guidance

Intuition and true inner guidance also have their beginnings in the first two chakras. Intuition is the soul's power of knowing God. It is a sixth sense, a "knowingness" which does not come to you from the five senses or even from the rational mind—it comes from your higher Self or superconsciousness.

For perfect intuition to develop there has to be clarity and strength of purpose and the centeredness of the positive side of the first chakra. Then with those qualities in place as a firm foundation, we can develop a freedom to flow with life's changes. The water element of the sacral chakra is where we begin to feel at home in the flow of life, accepting everything as it comes, with true discrimination and inner joy—knowing the thing to do and when to do it.

Meditation for the Water Element

Here are two kinds of meditation for the second chakra:

First, center your consciousness about an inch and a half above the base of the spine. Mentally chant AUM at that chakra. Look up at the point between the eyebrows. Feel the energy of the second chakra being directed upwards, toward that point.

Imagine yourself to be a flowing stream. As you pass through life, you touch many things, but are held by none of them. Your life keeps flowing onward toward the sea, the vast ocean of cosmic consciousness.

Now try it in another way: Yogis sometimes tell their disciples to stand in flowing water up to the neck and to meditate on, and identify themselves with, the water passing by them, or to imagine even that the water is flowing right through them.

Imagine yourself standing up to your neck in a river. The river gently flows around you. Whatever comes, let it come. Whatever passes by you, let it pass. You are free. You own nothing; you are owned by nothing. You own no one; no one owns you. Offer everything that you own into that flow, and let it be taken away. Be free and complete in yourself.

You might want to try actually floating on your back in

the sea or a lake and abandon yourself mentally to the flow of divine grace. Yogis suggest that when you come to a body of water, whether it's a stream, lake, river, or the vast ocean, to stop and sit for a while and meditate on the qualities of the water. Whether literally immersed in or floating on water, sitting by the water, or only visualizing water in any form, feel that you are flowing freely, fearlessly, with the stream of sparkling water. Or see yourself floating on a calm lake or rocking on gentle ocean swells, caring not where they take you, full of faith in the divine will.

Affirm mentally, with a sense of deep inner peace and freedom, "I flow ever freely with the tides of grace."

CHAPTER FOUR

❖

The Fire Element (Third Chakra)

"I throw all my passions and earthly pleasures on Thy sacrificial fire, as the offerings and oblations of my devotion to Thee. In Thy blessed light I shall burn all shadows and fears of my imagination. In Thy blessed light I shall remain awake forever."

—Paramhansa Yogananda,
  from *Whispers from Eternity*, 1929 Edition

Fiery Self-Control

The water element in us must be perfected, not only by approaching it with the inner stability of the earth element (first chakra), but also by channeling it into the dynamic enthusiasm for self-improvement that marks, at its best, the fire element (third chakra) within us. Otherwise our surrender to the tides of circumstance, though calm, will yet be too passive and will not carry us forward on the pathway to perfection.

As with all the chakras, the fiery element contains an inner and an outer side—positive and negative aspects—dependent upon which way the energy is flowing through the chakra. When rightly directed, this fiery energy is a necessary aid on the path to liberation. Wrongly directed however, it too, like the earth and water elements, is a cause of human bondage.

The fire element, if developed without reference to the stability of the earth element, or to the flowing, more easy-going quality of the water element, can manifest as a certain destructive ruthlessness. For where the earth element is inert, and the water element is adaptive, the fire element is very dynamic, a quality that can become overly aggressive if it is not properly tempered. The image springs to mind here of a screaming warrior riding through a village, burning and killing in an intoxication of zeal, unmindful of the suffering that he is bringing to countless innocent people.

The negative side of the third chakra can manifest as harshness, intolerance, cruelty, anger, lack of consideration for anyone else, or using power that one has finally learned to control to abuse or ride roughshod over others. Those caught in this aspect of the fire element may become dictators, ruthless bosses, or just manipulators.

The positive side of the fire element allows us to burn away all obstacles that keep us from the truth. It is the element of fiery self-control. An example of this is a story that Ramakrishna, a yoga master of India, used to tell.

In some of the regions in India where water is scarce, there are certain hours of the day when irrigation water is allowed to flow into each of the farmers' fields; then it is shut off and channeled into other areas.

On a particular day, two neighboring farmers were taking advantage of the flowing water, opening up passages for it to water all their crops. They both were working very hard and becoming very tired. At that point, each of their wives came out to the field and told them please to come in as lunch was ready—it was time to eat.

One of them said: "Well, I know I shouldn't, but what can I do? She wants me." So he went.

The second farmer said very forcibly to his wife: "What do you mean by asking me to stop for lunch? Don't you see I've got work to do? Leave me now, and let me finish!"

He worked very hard for many hours and made sure that the water reached all his crops. But the other farmer's crops failed for lack of sufficient water, and he and his family starved.

The meaning of Ramakrishna's story is that if you are truly devoted to your spiritual path, then you don't say: "Well, I did want to meditate, but inasmuch as you've asked me to go to the movies with you, what can I do but go?" If you really mean business, you're going to have that fiery determination which won't allow other people's opinions or suggestions to sway you or stand in your way.

Working with the fire element is similar to working with light. Directed energy is very necessary on the spiritual path. Being able to draw it into a tightly focused ray, like a laser beam, is no easy job! You've got to be a warrior in the name of self-discipline.

Concentration of Energy

When we work with the chakras, we are entering an inner laboratory. Once we begin, we have to change our whole approach to the way we think; we've got to direct our energy inwardly. We must completely re-structure our thought patterns if we are to be able to go into deep meditation.

Yogananda's techniques of meditation include the "Energization Exercises," which he called the cornerstone of his teachings and which have this important guiding principle: "The greater the will the greater the flow of energy." When we consciously direct energy to the muscles while tensing them, we become aware of the enormous amount of energy that is available to us. But that's only one side of it.

The next important principle of the Energization Exercises is: "Tense with will, relax and feel." We send the energy to the body with will power, and then try to feel the energy withdrawing from the body. The more energy we are able to send to the muscles, the more aware we are of that energy. Then, with that greater awareness, we learn also how to withdraw that energy from the body and "relax and feel." Relaxation is a key aspect of deep meditation—but relaxation while still being very aware, focused, and in no way passive, dreamy, or sleepy.

The real secret of success in this world is twofold: concentration and energy. The two really go together; they're parts of the same thing. We concentrate our energy. But first we need to be able to have energy!

Geniuses or people of power and success are always people of great energy. They're often people very inconvenient to be around because they've got *so much* energy. But a genius will never whine, "Well, I don't know, I think maybe, sort of . . . ." Imagine Michaelangelo saying lackadaisically, "Well, gee, Pope, maybe I'd like to paint the Last Judgment, but (sigh), I don't know. But, well, OK, I've got nothing better to do next Saturday. So . . . I guess maybe I might try." It's impossible to imagine him that way! It was a huge project! When he put his mind to it, he put his *whole* mind to it, and he nearly killed himself in the process. Perhaps he was a bit fanatical, but to do a thing well, it must be done with a huge outpouring of energy.

Swami Kriyananda tells of this needed level of energy: "I've found in writing something, I probably have to go through it at least fifty times before I'm satisfied. I remember that in writing my autobiography, *The Path*, I experienced one of the best tests I have ever had to go through—because it was so difficult. Difficult, because I felt a great burden of responsibility in representing what I understood of my guru, Paramhansa Yogananda. To misrepresent him was my constant fear. I kept trying to do everything I possibly could to make it better. Many times I felt tempted to throw in the towel. I drove myself to the point that, literally, I would stagger when I walked. It was a tremendous test, but in fact that is the way to do a job well.

"When I completed *The Path* I went away to India and spent time in seclusion. Once you finish a big project, then try to withdraw from it. Try to feel the source of the energy you were using; then offer it back up to God, the universal, creative source of all energy."

On the spiritual path we need fiery self-control, because we're putting a halt to habits that we've developed over countless incarnations. We've got to be determined to discipline ourselves like soldiers. We need to take the energy previously committed to those habits we no longer want inside, and direct it in a new way. How can we do that? Within this chakra we must begin to rise above body consciousness, and that requires learning to hold the body still!

One of Yogananda's disciples tells the story of how he and she were sitting out on the beach meditating. She was being eaten alive by little sand fleas. But she realized that she couldn't sit next to Master, who was sitting so absolutely rock-firm, and not be rock-firm too. So she willed herself to sit still. She said later that the experience gave her a great deal of will power from that time forward.

In everything that you do, do it with fire! Do it with energy! Do it with everything you've got! Many people think, "Oh, I don't want to be attached to anything, and therefore, I'll do everything half-heartedly." But then they meditate half-heartedly, too. Whatever you do, do it with all your will power and all your energy. Then relax and feel. Feel that energy within and the great Source from which it comes.

It is important to remember that this fiery control we're talking about is control over *our own* energy. It is not taking control over other people, or abusing or trying to force them in any way. It's not imposing our will or trying to inflict our energy on them. It is learning how to regain control over our own energy, so we can withdraw it and direct it upward in the astral spine in meditation.

Remember that this world is intended to be a battlefield.

We don't want to do battle in such a way as to hurt people, but we do have to be very strong in order to accomplish our spiritual goals. Many people don't see that point; they defer to others all the time, hoping to let other people do their spiritual work for them.

During the Great Depression, Yogananda often spoke of the importance of having this warrior-like quality, saying, "If I needed a job and didn't have one, I would shake the world until it had to give me one!" This was one of the primary attitudes that he brought to bear on his life he was a man of enormous will power. Yet he was also a man of non-violence, a man of peace.

In our work, in our play, in everything we do, we can bring into practice this inner fire quality. Again it must be emphasized that if we are to use these chakras in the right way, they all must offered up into higher consciousness.

Meditation for the Fire Element

In meditation, mentally cast all your limitations—of thought, desire, and self-will—into a divine fire to be melted and purified into cosmic wisdom and love. Affirm mentally, "I cast my thoughts, desires, and all past karma into Thy flames of love. Make me whole! Make me pure! Make me one with Thee!"

Visualize a fire either outside yourself or at the spiritual eye. Feel that you are offering into that fire all your attachments, all your faults. Review your day's activities and offer into the flames any wrong thought, any wrong deed. Feel them being burned away, joyfully! There's no pain in this kind of purifying fire, rather just an offering up through your own will power, of all ego, all fear, all attachment, anger, selfishness, and indifference. Feel your freedom as you release these things.

Search your heart for any kind of attachment. Reach in mentally and take it from your heart and throw it into that fire. Think of a shepherd in the mountains, walking through the brush all day with his sheep, picking up fleas or other kinds of little insects in his clothing. At night he then has to go through his clothes and find these vermin and throw them into his campfire. Likewise, in the evening go through your heart and see what new attachments you've picked up that day. What new feeling of remorse, what new sense of self-identity, what new sorrow, what new desires have attached themselves to you? Then burn them; purify them, offering them all up to God.

Now enter mentally into that purifying fire yourself. From outside it seems hot, but as you get into it, it feels cool, pleasant, joyful—burning up your pride, burning all sorrows, and all regrets. Everything is going up in flames and becoming free in the skies of Spirit until you feel that you have no definition at all except that infinite bliss.

Affirm mentally: "I am a great yogi. I am free. I am bound by nothing. I own nothing; nothing owns me. I own no one; no one owns me. Thou and I are one!"

*   *   *   *   *

One final note before we move on to the higher chakras.

The more a person lives a worldly life, the lower is what might be called his spiritual "center of gravity." The more spiritual a person is, the higher in the spine that center is located. In this way, the lower three chakras may be understood to relate more strictly to worldly consciousness; the upper three relate more to spiritual consciousness. If you want to spiritualize your consciousness, you should try to center your energy increasingly in the upper three chakras.

But then we might wonder, "How are the lower spinal centers to be awakened, if one's concentration is directed exclusively to the higher centers?"

The answer is that concentration on these higher centers generates a magnetism that attracts the energy to flow upward through the lower chakras. It is this upward flow of energy at the chakras that constitutes their awakening. By too much concentration on the lower chakras, the natural tendency would be for the spinal energy to flow downward. (In this case, it would be the lower chakras that generate the greater magnetism, drawing down toward themselves the energy in the upper chakras.)

But in any case it is not a question of exclusive concentration. In relation to one another, the upper triad of centers deserves more attention than the lower. Still each chakra, in relation to its own various outward functions, can be spiritualized better by concentrating more deeply at its source, than on its outward energy-flow.

Thus it is a good practice in meditation to chant "AUM"

mentally three times at each of the chakras, moving up and down the spine several times. In this way the energy becomes somewhat withdrawn from the outer body into the inner centers. Once you feel the energy in the chakras, draw it upward by concentrating especially at the sixth chakra, the point between the eyebrows.

CHAPTER FIVE

❖

The Air Element (Fourth Chakra— the Heart)

"What is love? Is it only ours?
Or does love whisper in the flowers?
Surely we, children of this world,
Could not love by our own powers."

—"What Is Love?"
    from *Songs of Divine Joy*, by Swami Kriyananda

Expansive Love

The fourth, or dorsal chakra (*anahata*), is located in the center of the chest near the heart. This chakra is represented by the element of air. Air has the qualities of expansiveness and freedom and represents that state of awareness that precedes material involvement. It is like the gaseous state of matter before the stars and planets are formed, and therefore before formal distinctions appear to suggest differences between one manifestation of matter and another. At this "air" stage of creation, although the presence of different chemical elements in the gases might preclude our speaking of them as essentially one and the same thing, the connection between them, at least, is obvious, as it is not on a more solid level of material creation. In human beings, the air element heightens our sense of kinship with life in its countless manifestations.

Directed downward through the lower elements, however, this sense of kinship becomes particularized. One tends to feel a specific affinity for this person or that thing, and, generally, less affinity for other people or other things. In this way, likes and dislikes gradually develop. By means of our likes and dislikes, the air element in us launches us on our descent into delusion.

Ultimately, it is on the neutralization of our likes and dislikes that spiritual realization depends. If we could but overcome them at their source, the other, lower, elements would cease to exert any hold on us. But because we are enmeshed in the material delusion, to work only on overcoming our likes and dislikes, ignoring the elemental channels of earth, water, and fire through which they manifest themselves, might result in too vague an understanding of the nature of our likes and dislikes.

To work on developing the air element, moreover, without first developing the virtues of the lower elements, might only make a person apathetic—a condition in which many religious persons in fact dwell, mistakenly believing that by their wan outlook they are demonstrating non-attachment. The air element in us must be rightly developed, not suppressed. It must be stabilized, freed from prejudices, and fired with enthusiasm by the lower elements. It must itself be offered into a higher, divine vision. In this way, human likes and dislikes can be transmuted into unconditional love, which is the positive manifestation of the sense of kinship with life.

It must be understood that at the pivotal point of the heart chakra, when the evolving soul-consciousness becomes centered in the air element, one finds oneself very delicately poised between divine liberation on the one hand, and further involvement in delusion on the other. For the air element is so refined in itself that it may seem to be wholly spiritual and pure. The love that one feels for others will seem beautiful, selfless, and serene. One's strong inclination at this point is to pour out divine love individually—to love this person for his gentle smile, that one for his humility, still another for his unfailing kindness, even a materially-minded person for his spiritual naïveté, so like the callow ignorance of a child!

Even pure, selfless love has its pitfalls, however, for if it becomes particularized—no matter how pure the sentiment at its inception—the trend is easily started that leads progressively toward involvement in material distinctions again. Do not trust the freedom that you feel, once this pure love manifests itself in you. Offer it up into the still finer ether element (fifth chakra), in which is felt not only one's divine kinship with others, but also an expanding, impersonal sense of the essential oneness of all life.

Sometimes people try to have that "air-like" kind of expansiveness and freedom by not being loyal to anything or anyone. But with this attitude they will not to be able to grow spiritually. If we want to expand our consciousness, we need to have the attitudes that will help us to expand in the most effective way.

For example, if you want to break a hole in a field of ice on a river, you can't take a very broad based object and expect to go through the ice at all points. Instead, you use a small, sharp pick and punch through the ice at one point. Once you've broken through the ice to the water beneath, then you can go anywhere you want to in the water. Similarly, if we try to break through this veil of delusion at all points at once, then our focus will not be sharp enough to generate the power we must bring to bear on what we're trying to accomplish.

We each need to choose our own personal attitude towards God, our own individual way of approaching Him. It's perfectly true to say that all paths lead to God, but the fact is, if you're in a building, you can leave it only through one door. You may admire all doors, you may respect all doors; but if you really want to get somewhere, you can only go through one of them.

Developing Divine Love

There was a man whom Paramhansa Yogananda accepted as one of his disciples. We might think that anybody with the good karma to meet a great master must be a very highly developed soul, but this particular disciple was not what might be called a saint. He had many faults, but he had great love for God and guru. Yogananda commented on this disciple saying, "That kind of love is what saves a person." In other words, it is more important to have the right desires—even if we haven't yet overcome our wrong desires.

He also told his disciples, "Don't worry about your faults; just think about whether you love God enough." It is far more important to develop the supreme virtue of loving God than to overcome all the faults in your nature. That one love, if it becomes strong enough, will absolutely transform all the vices, all the sins, and all the mistakes that you have made. And putting yourself in tune with God will give you that strength.

Remember that there can be darkness in a room for thousands of years but bringing a light into the room causes the darkness to vanish as though it had never been. No matter what we've done, the only thing that can finally save us is the light and love of God.

Unless we really love, and unless we give our heart's love to God, we won't be able to advance truly rapidly on the spiritual path. The heart chakra is where we must begin to unfold the heart's natural love and offer it up to the Divine.

Desire vs. Devotion

When we speak of love, we are speaking of the heart's capacity for two kinds of love: desire and devotion, both of which are rooted in the heart chakra. When the rays of the heart go outward, then the energy of desire is operative, and we become bound.

Each one of our little desires and attachments is like a cord going out from the heart, attaching itself to the object of its desire. Until it finds that object, this cord is like an octopus reaching out and trying to grab something. It will just keep trying until it finds the object of its desire. Once that desire has been found and satisfied, that cord or little ray of energy may cease to reach out from the heart. If that is indeed the case, one might think the way to find freedom is to just go out and fulfill all one's desires. It could work that way, but unfortunately it doesn't!

The reason is because, even when a desire is fulfilled, it usually gives birth to more desires! It is also because the memory of the pleasure of that fulfillment leads to the desire to experience that pleasure again.

What felt good was sort of like pinching your skin. You pinch it and pinch it and pinch it. Finally you let go, and it feels so good! Likewise, the fulfillment of a desire doesn't give us permanent joy. Why? Nothing can give us joy, because we *are* joy. Desires merely place conditions upon that joy that limit our ability to really enjoy anything. We place a condition on our happiness by saying, "I won't be happy until I get such and such." When we get it, we feel so good only because we're relieved, and we affirm the happiness that we had already in the first place. That's why some people can be happy with absolutely nothing, while other people can have everything materially and still not be happy.

When we try to fulfill material desires, we find that they just keep growing, and the opportunity for fulfilling them becomes smaller and smaller. The way out of this trap is to cut those cords, and to learn to re-direct that energy up toward the brain. When we can do that, then we achieve true freedom. Freedom doesn't mean doing just what we want to do, unless we understand that what we really want to do is become one with the Divine. We want to be in a divine flow. But if we allow ourselves to be drawn in to our egoic desires, we can never get into that flow, and never find what we really want in life.

If we can get into the consciousness of doing everything for and with God, and understanding that we only want to align ourselves with the divine will, then we will find that things always work out well. Giving energy to anything that goes in any other direction will always end up in pain for us. Remember that God's will for you is always for your true happiness.

Perhaps we imagine God's commandments as coming from a glowering God, who is standing there saying, "I command you to do this, and I command you not to do that!" Then we mutter, "Oh, all right (tyrant!)."

It is not that way at all! God is offering us those situations that are for our own highest welfare because it is the laws of our own true nature that are in operation. When we follow His way, then we find that even the cross leads to the resurrection. The greatest test that a human being can go through leads only to joy and a feeling that the test never really existed at all.

There is a lovely story from the life of a Sufi woman saint named Rabbi'a. She was in her old age, close to death, and in great physical pain, when three of her disciples came to console her.

"He is no true lover of God, after all," said one, "who is not willing to suffer for God's sake."

"This smacks of egoism to me," replied the saint. Another of the disciples attempted a correction: "He is no true lover of God who is not happy to suffer for God's sake."

"More than this is needed," she replied.

"Then you tell us, Mother," said the third. "What should be the right attitude for a lover of God?"

"He is no true lover of God," Rabbi'a said, "who does not forget his suffering in the contemplation of the Supreme Beloved."

God's will and God's presence in the divine flow of our lives makes nothing else exist for us. The little bit of pain we experience here in this world is well worth it. And even pain doesn't exist if we are in tune with God's will—in tune with the divine flow.

The only thing that works is to love God and to feel God's love for you. A great Catholic saint, St. Jean Vianney, the Curé d'Aar, once said, "If you only knew how much God loves you, you would die for joy!"

The first and most important thing on the spiritual path is to learn devotion, to give our love and our lives to God. If we can achieve that consciousness, then all the rest of our spiritual progress comes relatively easily. If you will open your heart to God, then you will find that there isn't anything He can't do for you and through you.

When we open ourselves to divine love, we naturally feel drawn to be serviceful to others and to God. One of the most helpful attitudes on the spiritual path is not to have the thought of doing things *for* God, but rather the thought of doing them *with* God. Make God your companion on the path. This attitude draws more grace into your life, because there is less of the thought of "I" in it, and more of the thought of allowing divine energy and love to flow through you.

The Meaning of Impersonal Love

It is very important on the spiritual path to develop a kind of impersonality in the way we love. This is not an easy concept to understand, and in the beginning it may even seem cold. Swami Kriyananda tells of times when Yogananda would seem very withdrawn and abstract. He says: "To my understanding he sometimes seemed cold or aloof. Yet I knew he couldn't really be cold, because he was a saint of love."

This seeming impersonality is often manifested by great saints and masters. For example, once Ramakrishna was in the temple at Dakshineswar performing a ceremony. Rani Rasmani was in attendance. She was the wealthy donor who had built the temple—in fact you could say she was his boss. During the ceremony she was thinking about a lawsuit she was involved in at that time.

Ramakrishna, who was functioning on a superconscious plane, knew what her thoughts were. He turned around and slapped her, saying, "Those thoughts in this house of God? How dare you!"

Everyone was all set to throw him out on his ear; after all, it's not a good thing to treat the boss that way. But she said, "No, he's right. Let him be."

Ramakrishna would never have done a thing like that deliberately, but while he was in a divine flow with his ego completely out of the way, something just happened over which he had no control.

The truth is very impersonal; therefore the true love we give each other should be more impersonal. That is why the Indian scriptures speak of the wife and the husband loving each other for God's sake—seeing God in each other, rather than just the other person. If we can learn to see that God is in everyone, in every situation, we will never suffer another disappointment. There will be no more pain for us, but only that joy of knowing God's presence.

There must always be some little corner of the heart that is reserved for God alone. As long as we get too personal with people, we'll be centered in them. We must become centered in ourselves, for it's inside that we will find God.

Now the other side might be represented by the traditional monastic attitude that tends to over-emphasize a person's non-involvement in life, or the impersonal, without any sweetness. Therefore, although they are impersonal, they are also cold. Instead we need to understand that we've got to do *everything* joyfully for and with God. We should not seek to remove our spiritual practices from our daily lives, thinking, "As long as I'm doing my work, and as long as I'm serving my children and my spouse, I'm not doing a spiritual thing. When I can get these duties out of the way, then I can have a few minutes with God." Rather we need to see and feel God's presence in every person, in every action, and in every moment of our day.

Feel all that you do in this world as an extension outward from your center and then bring it back to your center again. Realize that the pleasure you feel in enjoying things of the world is really primarily in the heart. When you see a beautiful sunset, don't let your heart leap outward to the sunset. Instead think, "Divine Mother, from within my own heart I appreciate what wonderful things You do!"

You'll find that if you have this internalization of consciousness, it allows you to take that joy inside and feel its divine source. The sweetness of life is constantly fed by your inner joy, and it becomes more and more beautiful.

Otherwise the time comes when anything in life can be boring. The most inspiring music, the most beautiful sunsets, the loveliest paintings—an excess of these things can become boring in the end, if we don't understand that the essence of our enjoyment of them comes from inside. If we experience even the most wonderful things to the point of satiety, our senses begin to feel assaulted by them. But when, in deep meditation, you hear the inner sound of AUM, you'll know that it's playing the heartstrings of your own being. You'll know that you could listen to it for all eternity and never get tired of it. That's the difference; the senses tire, but the soul never tires.

In your relationships with each other, even in your most intimate moments, feel the communion inside yourself, not outside. Then feel this communion going toward the impersonal, realizing that it's all really God.

Paramhansa Yogananda said that the spiritual path is like running a race and performing stunts along the way. It's a very tricky thing to find a balance on that fine razor's edge between what seem like opposites: personal and impersonal love.

However people treat us is, in fact, God treating us that way. If we accept this, then we will be able to accept them in a more loving way. We won't think of them in terms of what we can get from them, but only in terms of their welfare. When we are impersonal, then we have more love to give, not less, because we really think in terms of giving, not taking.

Another point we've touched on before, but which is important to emphasize, is that the heart's energy can go either upward or downward. When we feel a great soaring joy in our hearts, it would be wise always to tie that joy to the spiritual eye (sixth chakra). Meditation on the heart is a good thing, because it helps to stimulate love. But then that love must be directed toward and anchored in the point between the eyebrows. That way the energy won't slip into downward or outward channels. It is very easy for the thrill of love and freedom in the heart to take us into yet another error, if we don't turn it upward.

Whatever you do in life, always watch your heart. Watch your feelings. You'll notice that there is a real ray of energy, of force, going out from your heart toward people, things, or expectations. Learn to control and re-direct that energy. The more you direct it upward and offer it to God, the more you will find your every desire being fulfilled, always in the best possible way.

The unfolding of divine love in the heart chakra is the beginning of the true spiritual life. Without the awakening of divine love, the spiritual path is all lectures, books, noble ideas, fine resolutions, and strong affirmations—but no great change takes place. Once you really catch hold of divine love, then there isn't anything that you can't have. You are a child of God. It is your birthright to know Him and to merge back into Him, into His divine love.

Meditation for the Heart Chakra

Sit upright with a straight spine, shoulders back, and with your chest up and open. To relax your body, first inhale and tense the whole body, then exhale and relax completely. Do this three times. Now, inhale slowly and feel that you're filling your whole body with air, from the feet up to the top of the head. Exhale, and feel that you're expelling all tension, all impurity, and all worldly attachment. Inhale, filling the body with lightness and air, from the feet up to the top of the head. Exhale impurities and tension. Do this again, one final time.

Think of your heart, and visualize strings of attachment—cables, in some cases, threads in others—going out in all directions towards various objects. You don't need to think of the objects; just think of all those cords going out, attaching yourself to the things of the world. Imagine taking an ax, a saw, or some scissors (whatever you need) and cutting them away.

Mentally affirm: "With the sword of devotion I sever the heart-strings that tie me to delusion. With the deepest love, I lay my heart at the feet of Omnipresence."

Polish the heart till it shines and reflects back to the world only light and love. Then go inside the heart, and whatever little seeds of desire may still be there, pull them out with your fingers and cast them up into the air, allowing the wind to take them away. Your heart becomes as light as a balloon and can soar upward, free from the trammels of earth. Feel your heart soaring upward. All its rays of aspiration are turned toward freedom, toward the sky, toward the Infinite.

Now feel and meditate on the thought of the air element of your body. Your body is made of air; it is as light as air. Think of the freedom of the vast blue sky. Then visualize a balloon filled with helium, so it can fly upward. Think of this balloon as symbolizing all your likes and dislikes, all your worldly desires and attachments. Release the string of ego by which you hold this balloon in your grasp. Watch the balloon soar upward, growing smaller and smaller with distance, until it finally disappears into the air and only the vast blue sky is left. Your whole concentration is on being in the air, and having nothing left to concentrate on but air. You become the air itself.

Affirm quietly but joyfully: "Nothing on earth can hold me! My soul, like a weightless balloon, soars upward through skies of eternal freedom!"

CHAPTER SIX

❖

The Ether Element
(Fifth Chakra)

"My silence, like the ether, passes through every-thing, carrying the songs of earth, atoms, and stars into the halls of His infinite mansion."

—Paramhansa Yogananda
  From *Metaphysical Meditations*, 1932 Edition

Calmness and Expansion

The fifth chakra, the cervical or *vishudha* chakra, is the center which relates to the element of ether. The ether state symbolizes breaking through the final veils of delusion, helping us to realize that there is something beyond this ego and this personality, altogether. Ether is a very subtle element, which, in the past, scientists pretty well discarded as not having any reality. But a few scientists are beginning to look at this theory again in certain contexts—for example, observing that light does seem to move in some kind of a medium. Thus it seems we are coming full circle, to a place where there is some discussion in scientific circles that something, which might be called "ether," actually does exist.

Yogananda said that the vibration that separates the material universe from the astral universe is the vibration of space, or ether. Space is an actual vibration. He mentioned, for example, that for people who have been blind for many years and then are suddenly able to see again, through medical intervention or a miracle of some sort, their first impression is that everything is flat. There isn't anything farther and closer;

rather space is somehow a distinct vibration that makes it seem that way.

This concept is similar to what a great saint, Ramana Maharshi, said to a woman who came from London to visit him in India. She was remarking on how far she had come, and he said, "You haven't moved at all; the world moved around you." We are always at the center of whatever reality is. And in the last analysis, there isn't anything but that center. There is nothing big or small, here or there—it all just is.

In any case we are obviously talking about something very subtle. The subtlety of it also suggests the quality of consciousness that comes with the energy being awakened in this chakra. The inner qualities of the throat chakra are calmness and expansion.

Calmness differs from peace. Peace is an aspect of God, too, but it is that which you experience once the agitation of the mind is stilled. It's similar to a deep sleep from which you awaken feeling great. In deep sleep you've gotten back in touch with the chakras. The more you consciously withdraw your energy into the chakras through meditation, the more you experience an enormous revitalization of energy and consciousness.

An experience of inner peace is very pleasant—you feel as if you were standing under a waterfall, bathing yourself with peace. It's wonderful, refreshing, releasing. But there's another side to it also, which is very dynamic. When you get into a deeper level of calmness, what you begin to feel is something very powerful indeed. It is an expansion of consciousness that begins to take you away from the ego. It is almost overwhelming, much more than a simple state of peace might be. This profound calmness is the soil in which cosmic consciousness begins really to blossom forth in your consciousness.

The fifth chakra's outer side is the opposite of calmness—restlessness and boredom, mercurial and changeable. The influence of that aspect of consciousness takes us up and down, makes us restless, run around and do many things, and have many experiences as a way of fighting boredom. Remember that although deep meditation is very calming, it is not boring or threatening to all the things that we enjoy. It offers a much greater enjoyment!

Focusing on the inner aspects of this chakra leads us towards an exceptionally clear mind, a very keen understanding that cannot come without deep inner calmness. In our daily lives we should always try to be calm inside. Whatever you do, always feel that, in a sense, you are watching it happen—you are an interested but impartial observer. When you experience pain in this world, just say, "All right, this experience is happening and it is necessary. It will teach me lessons, but it won't last. Let it teach me at least to be non-attached to it."

Swami Kriyananda comments: "You will find very often that the seemingly negative experiences in life are the best ones for you. It's because of those pains, because of the tragedies, because of the intense disappointments we experience, that we get turned in a spiritual direction. I know that has been true for me, and I suspect it's true for everyone. If you take the painful experiences in the right way, instead of merely allowing them to make you bitter, you soon will be able to tell yourself, 'Oh, yes, I see that such is the nature of this world. I see that I can't rely on this world to give me everything that I want.'"

This was what Buddha experienced when he first saw an old man, an ill man, and finally a dead man. He saw that life is a very shaky proposition if it can hold the infirmity of age, the debility of sickness, and one's total inability to accomplish anything more when death comes.

In suffering we are reminded of the sorrows of many lives,

and we begin to long to turn toward the Divine. We need to recognize the good in both joy and sorrow, for both have much to teach us. In darkness, light is born. In silence, sound is born. It is because of the negative side that the positive is possible. We should be grateful for both, and yet be removed from both by becoming centered in ourselves, beyond duality in our oneness with God.

The Voice

This chakra affects the voice and speech. In fact, this is why the control of speech is a very important thing. Learn not to talk too much. Conscious silence gives us the opportunity to draw that otherwise outwardly directed energy within, stimulating this chakra.

We can also use the energy of the chakras in an outer way to awaken them, if we are aware of the qualities of their inner energy. For example, the voice is a reflection of our actual nature—our personality, our emotions and thoughts. Therefore, if you try to develop the speaking or singing voice in a conscious way—using it to express harmony and kindness—it will help develop the beneficial aspects of the throat chakra.

Listen to your own voice when you speak, and you will notice very quickly if there's any kind of consciousness that comes into it which sounds negative. For instance, whatever emotion you're feeling—anger, tension, egoism—you'll hear reflected in the voice. As the Bible says, "Out of the fullness of the heart, the mouth speaketh." (Luke 6:45) It is true in a literal sense—it's not just psychological and spiritual.

An interesting thing, which several saints have pointed out, is that one of the first things that a person develops as he or she takes up the practice of yoga is a sweet voice. Though this doesn't mean necessarily a singer's voice—that depends on the kind of physical "musical box" you've got—still, as you develop spiritually, the voice begins to develop a kind of beautiful sweetness.

To develop the fifth chakra, it would help you to use the voice in a divine way by trying to bless people through the tone of your voice. Try not to use your voice only as a sort of beast of burden for your ideas, but as a channel for calmness. You'll find that you really can change your own and other peoples' consciousness simply with the quality of your voice.

Singing Through the Chakras

Most singers are trained to use chest tones to add fullness to the voice. But you can also learn to sing "from the heart," which gives the music a markedly different and very devotional feeling. This concept is difficult to transmit through the written word, but you might listen to Swami Kriyananda singing or chanting on one of his albums—perhaps this would help you to understand this devotional quality better. With practice you can learn to sing through the throat chakra, the heart chakra, or through the spiritual eye. Each has its own unique and subtle vibration.

Kriyananda tells of an interesting experience he had in San Francisco, when he was recording an Indian mantra, "Sri Ram, Jai Ram."

"As I was recording it, I suddenly felt my energy going up into the throat chakra." I said to the recording engineer, "Let's do it again."

He said, "What do you mean? That was perfect!"

I said, "No, let's do it again."

Swami Kriyananda knew that it would sound different, calmer and more expansive, and it did. Later a curious thing happened. A friend of Swami's had a little child, two years old, who loved this particular recording of "Sri Ram." One day when she was scolding him, he looked up at her and sang in a wistful little voice, "Sri Ram, Jai Ram?" He had felt that expansion of peace, that calmness which had come through Swami Kriyananda's singing through the throat chakra, and now to offset her scolding, he hoped to convey that feeling to her.

The ether element, finally, is too subtle to be a cause of material bondage. It contains only the potential of worldly involvement, as invisible cosmic energy contains the potential for manifestation as matter. Yet it may be said that energy's potential for material manifestation differs from that of pure Spirit in the sense that it is more dynamic, more actual.

The ether element within us, similarly, represents that inner pause in which wrong, as well as right, directions may be determined. Inner calmness and the thought, "It's all one to me," so long as the mind is outwardly directed, may soon turn to boredom, and a desire for more active worldly involvement. The sense of the oneness of everything will be spiritual only when it is supported by an upward movement of consciousness from the lower chakras, and particularly by the feeling of selfless, divine love in the heart center. This expansive sense of oneness, finally, must itself be directed upward to the point between the eyebrows and to the universal divine vision of which that sense of oneness is only the foundation.

Meditation for the Ether Element

As your body is the little body, so God's body is space, and if you want to feel Him you must feel space in the body and all space beyond it. Close your eyes and feel space all around your body, stretching out in all directions to infinity. Feel that space becoming a vast sea of light in which you are floating. Feel that light coming into every part of your body, from the soles of your feet to the brain. Your body is now made of light, merged with the vast sea of light and space within and all around you.

Imagine yourself leaving this earth, flying upward into the vast blue sky, upward further still into outer space, toward the dim stars and distant skies lying beyond the eternal stillness of the ether. Joyfully leave everything behind you—all attachments, all that keeps you bound to this world.

Dwell in inner silence and mentally repeat: "My silence spreads like an expanding sphere, directionless, everywhere. My silence, like the ether, passes through everything, carrying the songs of earth, atoms, and stars into the halls of His infinite mansion." (From *Metaphysical Meditations*, by Paramhansa Yogananda, 1932)

CHAPTER SEVEN

❖

The Sixth and Seventh Chakras: Enlightenment and Liberation

"I will close my material eyes and dismiss the temptations of matter. I will peer through the darkness of silence until my eyes of relativity open into the one inner eye of light. When my two eyes of good and evil become single, and behold only the divine goodness of God in everything then I shall find my body, mind, and soul filled with His omnipresent light."

—Paramhansa Yogananda
From *Metaphysical Meditations*, 1932 Edition

The Medulla Oblongata

The highest center in the spine is the medulla oblongata, the negative pole of the *ajna* chakra. Its positive pole, the point between the eyebrows, is also known as the "single," "third" or "spiritual" eye, the Christ center, or, in Sanskrit, the *Kutastha Chaitanya*. The medulla oblongata is the center through which cosmic energy feeds the entire body, and is the receptive aspect of the sixth chakra.

It is from the medulla oblongata (also called the brain stem, or primitive brain, located in the lower part of the skull, just where it connects to the neck and spinal cord), Paramhansa Yogananda explained, that the sperm and ovum, when united, move outward to create the physical body. The energy, as it creates the body, moves upward from the medulla to the brain, and downward from the medulla through the spinal column, whence it radiates outward to form the nervous system and the body. The medulla oblongata is the seat of life in the body, and contains the only body part that cannot be operated on, except peripherally.

Yogananda taught, through his Energization Exercises, how to energize the body at will. For our bodies' energy doesn't depend on food, air, and sunlight alone. We live surrounded by an ocean of cosmic energy, and draw on it to a greater or lesser extent all the time, depending on our will power, or willingness, and on the clarity of our awareness. This energy enters our bodies just as it did in the creation of the body, through the medulla oblongata. For this reason, too, you will find it helpful during meditation to deepen your awareness of the medullary aspect of the sixth chakra.

Another important aspect of the medulla oblongata is that it is the seat of the ego, where the consciousness of most human beings is centered. Everything they do, think, and perceive is centered in ego-awareness, which originates from this point. The yogis explain that egoism is the primary cause of bondage. It is because of ego that desires infest the heart.

Yogananda defined the ego as the soul identified with the body. Soul freedom consists essentially of banishing this sense of ego by realizing that we are not the body, but the Infinite Spirit. Through meditation we gradually release this identification and find out who and what we really are: not the body or personality, but Infinite Spirit.

Yet the ego is our sense of self (the "little self" it is often called), which we must deal with appropriately, for it is extremely strong and cunning. It will not surrender itself into the

Higher Self until it is ready to do so and, indeed, is convinced that surrendering itself is in its best interests.

The Spiritual Eye

The consciousness of enlightened beings is centered in the Christ center between the eyebrows. All their actions, thoughts, and perceptions originate from that point, rather than from the seat of ego in the medulla.

The goal of all spiritual seekers is to get to the Christ center and live in that consciousness. To remain blocked in the medulla would only feed ego-consciousness. However, it is good and necessary to deepen one's awareness of the medulla first, since it is the point through which consciousness and energy must pass in order to reach the Christ center or spiritual eye.

By concentrating at the spiritual eye on the inner light, or upon any other divine reality that one actually perceives when the mind is calm, we gradually take on the qualities of that inner reality. The mind loses its ego identification, and begins to merge in the great ocean of consciousness of which it has always been a part.

Jesus, in Matthew 6:22, said, "The light of the body is the

eye: if therefore thine eye be single, thy whole body shall be full of light." Thus the passage reads in the Authorized, or King James, version of the Bible, and also in the original Greek. Modern translators from the Greek have, for the most part, changed that word, "single" (which gives the true meaning of the Greek, *haplous*), to read, "If your eye is sound." Some go even farther. They make "eye" plural. Thus, their translations read, "If your eyes are sound." They overlook a deep spiritual truth, however, in their effort to adjust the passage to what seems to them a more reasonable interpretation of its meaning.

The vision of the inner light comes in deep meditation. It is beheld in the center of the forehead, between the eyebrows. This is why saints in ecstasy are so often depicted gazing upward. Once the vision of light in the forehead takes shape, once the mind is deeply concentrated, it becomes what mystical tradition calls "the single eye," "the third eye," or, in yoga teachings, "the spiritual eye." The two eyes of the body behold the world with dual vision, and, therefore, in relativity. The eye of the soul, however, beholds all things as belonging to the sole Reality, God.

The spiritual eye is not imaginary. It is something one actually sees in meditation, when the thoughts are stilled, and when the intellect functions on its own higher, intuitive level.

When the spiritual eye is beheld perfectly, it is circular in shape even as the eyes of the body are behind their eyelids. It is seen as a ring of shining golden light surrounding a field of intense, deep blue or violet. In the center of the blue-violet field shines a brilliant, five-pointed, silvery-white star. When the spiritual eye is beheld imperfectly, it is seen as a dim violet light with a faint circle around it, and an even fainter dot in the center.

In meditation, concentrate at a point midway between the eyebrows. Close your eyes (or keep them half-open and half-closed) and look upward—not crossing your eyes, but converging them slightly as though you were gazing at your thumbnail outstretched above you. Don't be too exact in this matter, however. The important thing is to bring your attention to that area. Don't try forcibly to bring your eyes to a focus, but gaze mentally towards that point, and let the spiritual eye draw you into itself. At all times keep your eyes relaxed and your brow smooth.

Gaze deeply into, and behind, the darkness you behold at the point between the eyebrows when your eyes are closed. The more intently you gaze, with deep calmness, the sooner you will behold at the center of that darkness an island-like area of blue or violet light, surrounded, perhaps, by a faint circle of white or yellow. The light may be dim at first, but it will present the beginning of what will take shape, in time, as the spiritual eye, as described above. Remember not to strain. Rather, simply channel your awareness calmly, and with a feeling of joyous aspiration, to that point. Whether or not you behold the spiritual eye, by meditating at that point your consciousness will gradually rise until at last it passes the portals of human awareness and enters the state of ecstasy, or superconsciousness. In this state of ecstasy, the consciousness penetrates the spiritual eye and enters the inner realms.

Paramhansa Yogananda made it a deliberate practice to keep his mind centered at the Christ center throughout the day, regardless what his other activities were. He also told his disciples to do this, as much as possible, as a way to experience the divine very quickly.

One problem people face is not knowing from what position, mentally, to approach that spiritual center. Concentrate the attention first in the region of the medulla oblongata, and from that point gaze toward the spiritual eye. People's awareness of their egos is often distributed vaguely throughout the body. By centering it consciously in its true seat, the medulla, it becomes possible to direct ego-consciousness toward its own higher octave. Once ego-consciousness has been dissolved in superconsciousness, one's consciousness soars upward through the spiritual eye and out into Infinity.

Spiritual Eye Meditation

Concentrate at the point between the eyebrows. Visualize there a tunnel of golden light. Mentally enter that tunnel, and feel yourself surrounded by a glorious sense of happiness and freedom. As you move through the tunnel, feel yourself bathed by the light until all worldly thoughts disappear.

After soaring through the tunnel as long as you feel to do so, visualize before you a curtain of deep violet-blue light. Pass through that curtain into another tunnel of deep, violet-blue light. Feel the light surrounding you. Slowly, the tunnel walls disappear in blue light. Expand your consciousness into that light—into infinite freedom and bliss. Now there is no tunnel. There is only the all-encompassing blueness and bliss of infinity.

At last, visualize before you a silvery-white, five-pointed star of light. Surrender every thought, every feeling into this star of absolute, ever-existing bliss.

Mentally affirm: "I awake in Thy Light, I awake in Thy Light, I am joyful, I am free, I awake in Thy Light!"

The Seventh Chakra and the Goal of Samadhi

The seventh and highest chakra, located at the top of the brain, is known as the *sahasrara,* or thousand-petaled lotus. This is the highest chakra. All the rays of the brain go out from that point, and it is at the thousand-petaled lotus that the soul finally becomes united with God.

Though it is the highest center, it must be approached through the Christ center (sixth chakra)—you can't really reach the seventh chakra until the spine has been completely magnetized in the lower six chakras. In that magnetizing process, and by prolonged meditation on the spiritual eye, a subtle passage automatically opens up from that center to the top of the head. To attempt to approach the *sahasrara* by any other route would be futile; it has even been said to be dangerous, for it can disrupt the flow of energy between the medulla and the crown chakra. The proper pathway is through the spiritual eye. It is important to understand that the spiritual eye is the seat of enlightenment and the crown chakra is the seat of liberation. You must become enlightened first, in order to become liberated.

The goal of all yoga practices is samadhi or superconscious

union of the little self with the Higher Self or God. Samadhi comes after one learns to dissolve his ego consciousness in the calm inner light. Once the grip of ego has really been broken, and one discovers that he is that light, there is nothing to prevent him from expanding his consciousness to infinity. The devotee in deep samadhi realizes the truth of Christ's words, "I and my Father are one." The little wave of light, losing its delusion of separate existence from the ocean of light, becomes itself the vast ocean. Just as a wave melts in the sea, so the human soul melts into Spirit.

At first, the ego's addiction to a separate existence allows the soul only brief flights of ecstasy before selfhood reasserts itself. The bird, imprisoned for eons in its little cage, fears to come out even though the door of the cage stands wide open. After a time, deciding that no threat is posed by that openness, the bird hops briefly outside—two or three hops, only—fluffs its wings, then hops hurriedly back to the reassurance of its cage again. Again it hops out, and ever and again returns, still preferring its delusive security to freedom. Then at last it begins to think, "Outside the cage is where I really belong!" At last, taking courage, it leaves its cage altogether, and flies outward to embrace the freedom it had so long denied.

Final emancipation is attained when all the old seeds of

karma have been destroyed. Buddha, Jesus Christ, Krishna, and others, including several great masters of modern times, attained this final state of emancipation. Only when the soul is convinced down to its last layer of consciousness that it is free is final liberation attained.

Samadhi may seem distant and even unapproachable from where we feel ourselves to be at this moment. But the simple thought that we are not free is what keeps us from being free! If we could break even that one idea, we would go into samadhi. Samadhi is not something we have to acquire. In truth, we have it already; we just haven't fully realized it. Train your mind to think in this way: "Eternally we have been with God; for a short time we are in delusion, then again we are free in Him forever."

Paramhansa Yogananda was equally at home on all levels of reality. Swami Kriyananda recalls with amazement how effortlessly Yogananda would enter samadhi. "For most of us struggling devotees it takes time even to touch the hem of superconsciousness. For him, the vastness of cosmic consciousness was only a breath away. No environment was wholly mundane to him. Everywhere he saw God."

"Do you know where I wrote my poem, 'Samadhi'?" Yogananda asked his disciples one day. "It was on the New

York subway! As I was writing, I rode back and forth from one end of the line to the other. No one asked for my ticket. In fact," he added with a twinkle, "no one saw me!"

Paramhansa Yogananda often told his disciples: "Memorize my poem, 'Samadhi,' and repeat it daily. Visualize yourself in that infinite state; identify yourself with it in order to awaken within you that lost memory of what you are in reality: children of Infinity. For that alone is what you really are."

"Samadhi"

—From *Whispers from Eternity*
by Paramhansa Yogananda, 1949

Vanished the veils of light and shade,
Lifted every vapor of sorrow,
Sailed away all dawns of fleeting joy,
Gone the dim sensory mirage.
Love, hate, health, disease, life, death,
Perished these false shadows on the screen of duality.
Waves of laughter, scyllas of sarcasm, melancholic
　　　whirlpools,
Melting in the vast sea of bliss.
The storm of maya stilled

By magic wand of intuition deep.
The universe, forgotten dream, subconsciously lurks,
Ready to invade my newly wakened memory divine.
I live without the cosmic shadow,
But it is not, bereft of me;
As the sea exists without the waves,
But they breathe not without the sea.
Dreams, wakings, states of deep turiya sleep,
Present, past, future, no more for me,
But ever-present, all-flowing I, I, everywhere.
Planets, stars, stardust, earth,
Volcanic bursts of doomsday cataclysms,
Creation's molding furnace,
Glaciers of silent x-rays, burning electron floods,
Thoughts of all men, past, present, to come,
Every blade of grass, myself, mankind,
Each particle of universal dust,
Anger, greed, good, bad, salvation, lust,
I swallowed, transmuted all
Into a vast ocean of blood of my own one Being!
Smoldering joy, oft-puffed by meditation
Blinding my tearful eyes,
Burst into immortal flames of bliss,

Consumed my tears, my frame, my all.
Thou art I, I am Thou,
Knowing, Knower, Known, as One!
Tranquilled, unbroken thrill, eternally living, ever new
  peace!
Enjoyable beyond imagination of expectancy, samadhi
  bliss!
Not a mental chloroform
Or unconscious state without willful return,
Samadhi but extends my conscious realm
Beyond the limits of the mortal frame
To farthest boundary of eternity
Where I, the Cosmic Sea,
Watch the little ego floating in me.
The sparrow, each grain of sand, fall not without my sight.
All space like an iceberg floats within my mental sea.
Colossal Container, I, of all things made.
By deeper, longer, thirsty, guru-given meditation
Comes this celestial samadhi.
Mobile murmurs of atoms are heard,
The dark earth, mountains, vales, lo! molten liquid!
Flowing seas change into vapors of nebulae!

Aum *blows upon the vapors, opening wondrously their*
  veils,
Oceans stand revealed, shining electrons,
Till, at last sound of the cosmic drum,
Vanish the grosser lights into eternal rays
Of all-pervading bliss.
From joy I came, for joy I live, in sacred joy I melt.
Ocean of mind, I drink all creation's waves.
Four veils of solid, liquid, vapor, light, *
Lift aright.
Myself, in everything, enters the Great Myself.
Gone forever, fitful, flickering shadows of mortal memory.
Spotless is my mental sky, below, ahead and high above.
Eternity and I, one united ray.
A tiny bubble of laughter,
I am become the Sea of Mirth Itself.

---

*The yogi who has entered into *samadhi* finds that solids melt into liquids, liquids into gaseous states, these into energy, and energy into cosmic consciousness. He lifts the four veils of solids, liquids, gases and energy (the elemental aspects of the chakras), and finds the Spirit, face to face. The yogi, instead of finding cessation of life and joy, becomes the fountainhead of eternal bliss and life. The tiny bubble of laughter becomes the sea of mirth itself. By knowing God, one does not lose anything, but gains everything.

CHAPTER EIGHT

❖

The Colors and Sounds of the Chakras

"Hello there sister dewdrop,
Linger a little while!
Your colors in the sunlight
Would make a monarch smile.
What need have I for treasures:
Diamonds or gold?
The sweetest of all pleasures
Are here to behold!"

—"Hello There Brother Bluebell,"
from *Songs of Divine Joy*, by Swami Kriyananda

Colors

There is an ancient tradition in India that the chakras manifest progressively the colors of the rainbow. The lowest chakra represents red, the next one (second) orange, the third yellow, the next one (the heart chakra) green, the fifth (throat chakra) blue, the spiritual eye and the crown chakra, indigo and violet. The lowest vibration, of course, is red; this chakra is where the energy is going outward more. Violet is the highest vibration; it represents that aspect of the chakras that brings everything into a state of peace. The gradual spiritualizing process flows in the direction from the lowest chakra (red) to the highest chakra (violet). We tend to think of the cooler colors, violet and blue as more spiritual than the highly energized colors of red and orange.

Meditating on the chakras and their colors may help you to become more aware of the chakras. This information on the colors of the chakras is not being offered to you as a deep teaching. It is not something that Paramhansa Yogananda said; but it's an intriguing theory, and it's something interesting to play with. After all we have to have some fun!

Color therapy is a fascinating study, with techniques like "color breathing" and "bathing" in a colored light. A Buddhist priest from Thailand, who was also a healer, told Swami Kriyananda once that he had found in his experiments that putting people under a blue light would reduce their blood pressure by as much as twenty points. Putting them under a red light, would cause it to go up as much as twenty points.

You might try experimenting for yourself. Look at a pure color and absorb the color in through your eyes. Try breathing in the essence of the color. When you look at it, inhale and feel you're drawing that color into your consciousness.

Why are we attracted to different colors? Because they express what we are! Sometimes you see someone in a color and you just know that it is totally inappropriate for that person. And it's not because of the color of his eyes, skin, or hair, necessarily, though that may have something to do with it. But very often you don't know the color of the eyes or he or she is too far away for that to be really a part of the color scheme. You just feel that the color isn't right for the person, or that another color would be. Why? Because the color is not reflecting that person's spiritual state. We choose colors for ourselves for the same reasons—there are some times when you may feel attracted to yellow, sometimes to brown and heavy colors, sometimes to light pastel colors; this attraction will always reflect something of your inner consciousness.

We've discussed meditating on the chakras and on the internalization of their qualities. It might be interesting also for you to meditate on the color of those qualities. This is the essence of gem therapy too—an ancient yogic teaching that the color produced by light passing through a gemstone onto your body is very helpful for your body, your aura, and for your consciousness. (An explanation of the specific gemstones for each chakra and their colors is included later in this chapter).

There are some colors that you just drink in joyfully! All aspects of the color spectrum are joyful when they're pure! If you put a crystal in the sun and then allow the colors to strike your eyes, the thrill that you get in looking at the pure red is just as great as the thrill you get in looking at the pure blue, or the pure violet. Thus it is that the chakras are all very spiritual if we focus on their pure side, their inner side, rather than their outward manifestation.

Wearing bright, clear, cheerful colors is a service to everyone. Swami Kriyananda observes the colors people wear and says, "Often I will compliment someone, whether or not I know him or her, on the way they are dressed, especially the colors they are wearing. It is uplifting to look at them! Be aware of the effects that the colors you wear have on yourself and others.

"I'm happy to see people wearing more bright colors or

beautiful pastels these days, as opposed to dark, muddy colors or black. I've been told that black is fashionable as it has a 'slimming' effect, which is why women often choose it. But I say to that: 'Who wants to be around a bunch of scare-crows, anyway?'"

It is important to be conscious of the effect of the colors in your environment —furniture, rugs, walls—on your consciousness also. Blues, indigos, and violets are nice for a temple or meditation space. The greens of nature are calming and healing to the heart. The warming colors of red, orange, and yellow are obvious energizers. Any pure, clear color is good for the spirit. Whenever you see colors that you like especially, absorb them into yourself; let them vitalize your aura. An attraction to a particular color may suggest a need for it, as the craving for a particular food may indicate elements that are lacking in one's diet.

Metals and Gemstones

If you study the teachings of yoga for many years, you will become aware that there are countless mysteries in nature and in the human body. One such mystery is the value of wearing certain gems or metals next to the skin. The chapter called "Out-witting the Stars" in Yogananda's well-known book, *Autobiography of a Yogi,* describes this ancient and subtle therapy.

All things are made of vibrations, and have their own magnetic properties. Certain pure gems and minerals emit radiations that are beneficial to the body of man. One such "bangle" made of gold, silver, and copper was recommended by Yogananda for general use. He said that this bangle had more than physical value. He once advised a disciple, who was prone to having accidents, to obtain and wear one of these bangles.

Pure, unflawed gemstones of not less than two carats may also be beneficial, if set by a jeweler in such a way that the stones actually touch the skin. An armlet of general usefulness, but one that is too costly for the average person to buy, is the *navaratna,* or nine-stone bangle. It is composed of the following pure gemstones, each of them two carats or more: diamond, emerald, yellow sapphire, chrysoberyl cat's-eye, blue sapphire, hessonite or cinnamon garnet, coral, pearl, and ruby. Each of these stones represent one of the nine planets in our solar system.

Knowledge of one's own horoscope, and of the right stones to wear in order to strengthen weak planets and to offset the vibrations of inauspicious planets, is believed to be beneficial. If all you need personally is one or two stones, you may be able to afford such a bangle even if you are not wealthy. But to know which stones you need, you must have your horoscope converted from the normal Western astrological system to Indian sidereal or Vedic astrology—an important point to know, if you want to make proper use of this Indian science of gem therapy.

The information included here about the colors, metals, gemstones, and so on may be interesting and is certainly fun to know about; it can be applied creatively in many aspects of our lives. But remember that the real work in the chakras comes through sending the energy inward and upward through the chakras, magnetizing the astral spine and spiritual eye through meditation, opening the heart through devotion and selfless service, and shifting the attitudes in each chakra from the negative, downward and outward flow to the positive, inward and upward flow.

Remember, too, that it is important not to assess the value of your meditations or measure your spiritual progress by whether or not you experience phenomena, such as colors or sounds that may or may not come to you. Paramhansa Yogananda said: "The path to God is not a circus." Rather, observe how you are changing as a person in daily life. As one great saint put it: "Your religion is tested best in the cold light of day."

The Inner Sounds

The chakras also manifest different sounds. Remember that they are made of energy, which is vibrating at different frequencies. Wherever there is vibration, there is also sound, even if it is very subtle. When meditating deeply, you will begin to hear the subtle sounds of the chakras in an intuitive or inward way.

The energy emanating from the lowest chakra is like the sound of a bumblebee; or, if you hear it imperfectly, it may sound like a motor. But in any case, as with all the sounds of the chakras, it is an absorbing, inward kind of sound.

Once Yogananda was sitting in a room with his disciple, Dr. Lewis. Dr. Lewis was at the other end of the room, and Master said, "Listen!"—The motor-sound of his coccyx chakra was so strong that Dr. Lewis could hear it all the way across the room.

The sound of the second chakra is that of a flute. It might also be heard as water flowing over rocks in a small stream.

The energy from the third chakra makes a sound as of a plucked stringed instrument—the vina, they call it in India, but in the West we might liken it to a harp sound.

The heart center sounds like a deep gong or bell.

The throat chakra emanates the sound of wind in the trees, a very soothing and expansive sound.

The medulla is a combination of all these sounds. The sound here could be described as a roaring ocean or a bursting sea, and that vibration approaches very near to AUM itself.

In meditation, at the point when you begin to hear the inner sounds, your spiritual attunement becomes much stronger. It is not appropriate to further explain here the details of the AUM technique of meditation, or the other techniques of the path of Kriya Yoga as taught by Yogananda. If you are interested in learning more about these specific techniques, please see the *Resources* section at the end of this book.

Another way to awaken the chakras through the power of sound is the practice of chanting the sacred mantra of AUM at each individual chakra, starting with the G-note below middle C for the first chakra. Chant AUM, working your way up through the musical notes to the spiritual eye (for the exact notes, see the Chakras chart on page 120). Chant the sound as "OM-M-M," especially drawing out the "m-m-m" sound at the end and letting it vibrate deep within the chakra. Repeat this practice several times up and down the spine, ending at the point between the eyebrows. Close by sitting quietly in meditation, feeling new power and energy in the astral spine and the chakras, then offering it all back to its source in Divine Spirit.

Meditation for All the Chakras

In an ancient scripture of India, the *Srimad Bhagavatam*, Krishna teaches a technique for opening the lotus flowers at each chakra, which is a good meditation to practice.

Relax, and sit comfortably in any meditation pose. Take a few deep breaths. Inhale and tense the whole body, then throw the breath out and relax. Imagine a current coming up the center of the spine very slowly from the base (first chakra) to the medulla oblongata and then through the brain to the point between the eyebrows. The duration of this ascent should be not less than one minute. Feel each chakra as you draw the current through it; mentally chanting AUM three times in each chakra, and visualizing the rays from that chakra turning upward toward the brain. Visualize each chakra as a lotus blossom, with its petals symbolizing its rays of energy, first pointing downward. As you pass the energy through each chakra in turn, visualize the lotus blossom turning its petals upward, offering its energy into the next chakra above it. Then sit mentally chanting AUM at the spiritual eye, feeling the magnetization of the whole astral spine and the chakras, in all their radiant beauty, filled with Divine Light.

CHAKRAS CHART

	English Name and Location	Sanskrit Name	Body Areas and/or Functional Influences	Elements (Elemental Stages of Development)	Musical Note for Chanting AUM at Each Chakra
7th	Crown Chakra, 1,000-petaled lotus, at the top of the head	Sahasrara	Seat of the soul, site of liberation, comes only after enlightenment takes place at the 6th chakra		
6th	Spiritual or 3rd Eye; Christ Consciousness Center, at the point between the eyebrows	Ajna (positive pole)	Seat of enlightenment, divine guidance, intuition, concentration, and willpower	Super-ether	G (above middle C)
	Medulla oblongata, "Mouth of God," at the base of skull in the brainstem area	Negative pole of the Ajna chakra	Entry point of life-force (prana) regulates the breath and heartbeat, seat of the ego		F
5th	Cervical Center (Throat/Neck)	Vishudha	Neck, vocal cords, throat, oral communication	Ether	Eb (E-flat)
4th	Dorsal Center (Heart)	Anahata	Heart, lungs, breasts, diaphragm, circulation, arms, hands, manual dexterity	Air	D
3rd	Lumbar Center (Navel)	Manipura	Stomach, intestines, many organs of digestion and assimilation	Fire	Bb (B-flat)
2nd	Sacral Center (Sex Organs)	Swadisthana	Sexual organs, reproductive system, procreation	Water	A
1st	Coccyx Center (Base of Spine)	Muladhara	Legs & feet, walking, anus & elimination	Earth	G (below middle C)

CHAKRAS CHART (cont.)

	Beneficial (Positive) Qualities	Harmful (Negative) Qualities	Inner Sounds	Colors	Vedic Astrological Signs and *Ruling Planet*	Metals and *Gemstones*
7th	Beyond duality and all opposites, harmony, true omnipresent, omniscient, *samadhi* bliss			Violet		
	Attunement, radiant joy, solution-consciousness, strong will-power	Too intellectual or coldly rational	AUM (Om), like the roar of a great, bursting sea		Leo *Sun*	Gold *Ruby*
6th	Selfless service, divine surrender, little self offered into Higher Self	Ego-involved, proud, vain, too much focus on "I, Me, Mine"		Indigo	Cancer *Moon*	Silver *Pearl*
5th	Expansive, deeply calm, silence	Restless, bored, "spacey," mercurial, worldly longings	Wind in the trees, rushing water	Blue	Gemini Virgo	Mercury *Emerald*
4th	Devotion, divine love, unconditional love, compassion	Attachment & harmful emotions out of control (anger, rage, hatred, etc.)	Deep bell or gong (or higher bells)	Green	Libra Taurus *Venus*	Copper *Diamond*
3rd	Zest for life, enthusiasm, self-control, loving leadership	Ruthlessness and abuse of power	Harp, vina, plucked string instrument	Yellow	Aries Scorpio *Mars*	Iron *Coral*
2nd	Flexible, open, willingness to change, intuitive, creative	Wishy-washy, indecisiveness	Flute (crickets, trickling water)	Orange	Sagittarius Pisces *Jupiter*	Tin *Yellow Sapphire*
1st	Steadfastness, courage, loyalty, perseverance	Stubborn, bigoted, heavy-minded	Bumblebee (rumbling motor)	Red	Aquarius Capricorn *Saturn*	Lead *Blue Sapphire*

*Ida - Upward current on the left side of the spine; gemstone: cinnamon (hessonite) garnet
*Pingala - Downward current on the right side of the spine; gemstone: chrysoberyl catseye

About the Author

Savitri Simpson has taught classes and workshops on the chakras for nearly 25 years. She has served as a counselor, minister, and teacher at The Expanding Light Retreat Center where she also served as the director of the Ananda Yoga Teacher Training Program and is presently the director of the Ananda Meditation Teacher Program. She has a Bachelor of Arts Degree from Baylor University, Waco Texas. In addition to her primary devotion to yoga, meditation, and all related subjects, she is a musician, herb gardener, gourmet cook, and nature lover. She lives with her husband, Sudarshan and her cat, Grayson in a dome-home at Ananda Village near Nevada City, California.

About the *for Starters* series

❖

The "*. . . for Starters*" series was created to give both beginning and long-time practitioners a brief yet thorough introduction to some of the most popular spiritual topics and practices of our day. More than mere overviews, the books in this series will help you quickly gain a foothold of understanding—and even more importantly—they will help you find the enthusiasm and energy necessary to incorporate these principles and practices into your daily life. That is, they actively help you get started.

Titles in the "*for Starters*" series

Meditation for Starters
J. Donald Walters

Meditation brings balance into our lives, providing an oasis of profound rest and renewal. Doctors are prescribing it for a variety of stress-related diseases. This award-winning book offers simple but powerful guidelines for attaining inner peace. Learn to prepare the body and mind for meditation, special breathing techniques, ways to focus and "let go," develop superconscious awareness, sharpen your willpower, and increase intuition and calmness. Taught by J. Donald Walters, an internationally respected spiritual teacher who has practiced meditation daily for over fifty years. *Meditation for Starters* is available as a book & CD set, book & cassette set, and as a video. Each item is also sold separately.

Yoga for Starters
Gyandev McCord

A unique and innovative introduction to this popular topic, *Yoga for Starters* is a handy lay-flat reference book that covers the basic principles of yoga. Includes sections on standing poses, relaxation poses, spinal stretches, inverted and sitting poses, all with photographs. Also includes suggestions for routines of varying lengths from beginning to advanced study. Most importantly, *Yoga for Starters* gives a broad overview of what yoga is and the main principles and practices associated with it. In addition to a section on yoga postures, there are also chapters on yoga philosophy, breathing, healing principles, and meditation.

Intuition for Starters
J. Donald Walters

Every day we are confronted with difficult problems and thorny situations for which we either don't have enough information to make clear-cut decisions or for which there is no easy intellectual answer. At these moments, we all wish that there was another way to know how to make the right choice. Fortunately, there is another way: through using our intuition. More than just a "feeling" or a guess, true intuition is one of the most important—yet often least developed—of our human faculties. Often thought of as something vague and undefinable, many people mistakenly assume that intuition cannot be understood and developed. *Intuition for Starters* will explain what true intuition is, where it comes from, the practices and attitudes necessary for developing it, and how to tap into intuitive guidance at will.

Vegetarian Cooking for Starters
Blanche Agassy McCord

Interest in vegetarian eating has been exploding across the country over the last decade. Even many of those who may not want to eat a completely vegetarian diet now recognize that healthy living requires the incorporation of at least some vegetarian principles and foods into their diets. Yet, many of us are still confused by the different theories, fads, and techniques championed by various proponents of healthy eating. In *Vegetarian Cooking for Starters*, Blanche McCord gives straightforward, easy-to-follow dietary advice, immediately useful explanations on how to prepare basic ingredients for cooking, and simple but delicious recipes that will quickly help you incorporate vegetarian meals into your diet.

Index

❖

Index

Index

Resources

❖

Additional Selections from Crystal Clarity

The Art and Science of Raja Yoga
Swami Kriyananda

The Art and Science of Raja Yoga contains fourteen lessons in which the original yoga science emerges in all its glory—a proven system for realizing one's spiritual destiny. Absolutely unique, this is the most comprehensive course available on yoga and meditation today. Over 450 pages of text and photos give the reader a complete and detailed presentation of yoga postures, yoga philosophy, affirmations, meditation instruction, and breathing techniques. Also included are suggestions for daily yoga routines, information of proper diet, recipes, and alternative healing techniques. *The Art and Science of Raja Yoga* comes with an audio CD that contains: a guided yoga postures sessions, a guided meditation, and an inspiring talk on how the reader can use these techniques to solve many of the problems of daily life.

Awaken to Superconsciousness
Meditation for Inner Peace, Intuitive Guidance, and Greater Awareness
J. Donald Walters

Many people have experienced moments of raised consciousness and enlightenment—or superconsciousness—but do not know how to purposely enter such an exalted state. Superconsciousness is the hidden mechanism at work behind intuition, spiritual and physical healing, successful problem solving, and finding deep, lasting joy. Walters shares his knowledge of the ancient yoga tradition, explains how to apply yoga principles to daily life, describes how to attain inner peace, and provides inspiring meditative exercises.

Autobiography of a Yogi—Original Edition
Paramhansa Yogananda

Followers of many religious traditions have come to recognize this book as a masterpiece of spiritual literature. Yogananda was the first yoga master of India whose mission it was to live and teach in the West. His first-hand account of his life experiences includes childhood revelations, stories of his visits to saints and masters in India, and long-secret teachings of Self-realization that he made available to the Western reader. This highly prized verbatim reprinting of the original 1946 edition is the only one available free from textual changes made after Yogananda's death. Experience all its inherent power, just as the great master of yoga first presented it.

MUSIC FROM CLARITY SOUND & LIGHT

Music to Awaken Superconsciousness
Experience Inner Peace, Intuitive Guidance, and Higher Awareness
Donald Walters

Each of the lush instrumental selections on this recording is designed to help listeners more easily access higher states of awareness: deep calmness, intuition, joy, radiant health, and transcendence. Instruction in the liner notes guides listeners on how to actively achieve supercsonsciousness; or, it can be used simply as background music for relaxation and meditation.

Relax
Meditations for Piano
David Miller

Let peace gently enfold you as you listen to these lilting melodies. This soothing instrumental music is the perfect antidote to stress of all types. Calming and inspiring, it will lift you above day-to-day worries and cares. Play it after work, before falling asleep or anytime you want to banish tensions and troubles.

Secrets of Love
Melodies to Open Your Heart
Donald Walters

Unlike any music you have ever heard, *Secrets of Love* will transform your life. Each musical selection captures the essence of one of the many aspects of love. Perfect as background music, "mood" music, or music for relaxation, all eighteen songs can also be actively used as dynamic tools for awakening the loving qualities within your heart.

Mystic Harp 2
Derek Bell

Derek Bell is the legendary harpist of The Chieftains. Original melodies by Donald Walters capture the mystical quality of traditional Celtic music. Derek plays Celtic harp on each of the twenty richly orchestrated melodies. A beautiful sequel to the first Bell/Walters best-selling collaboration, *The Mystic Harp*.

Aum: Mantra of Eternity
Kriyananda

Continuous vocal chanting of AUM, the cosmic vibration of spirit in creation, blended with a rich tamboura accompaniment.